DOG BUTTON TRAINING LOGBOOK
Track Your Dog's Words, Progress, and Milestones

A companion journal to

Dog Button Training: Teach Your Dog to Talk — A Practical Guide to Button Communication

by

Karen E. Mueller, DVM

K. Mueller Publishing

This Logbook Belongs To:

Name(s):________________________________

Dog's Name:________________________________

Replace this photo with one of your dog.

This logbook is intended to be used for one dog.
If you are training more than one dog, a separate logbook is
recommended for each.

A Small Bonus to Support Your Journey

This logbook includes a free bonus resource created to support your button journey. It's designed to be used alongside this book, offering extra reassurance, examples, and gentle guidance as you practice.

Details on how to access the bonus are included at the back of the book.

Before You Begin

This logbook is designed to be used in sequence, reflecting how button training unfolds over time. The daily log pages and progress checklists work together to help you build skills gradually, notice patterns, and reflect on progress as it develops.

Button training is most effective when it's practiced consistently. If life gets busy or you take a break from training, simply take your time with the logbook as well. There's no need to rush ahead—progress is measured by understanding, not by the calendar.

This logbook is meant to support real learning, at a realistic pace.

How to Use This Logbook

This logbook is organized to support your button-training journey with structure, clarity, and encouragement. Rather than focusing on perfection, it helps you notice patterns, track progress, and stay oriented as your dog learns to communicate.

It is intended to be used for one dog. If you are working with more than one dog, a separate logbook is recommended for each.

Daily Log Pages

Use the daily log pages to record individual training sessions or meaningful moments with the buttons.

You can note which buttons were available or used, the context around each press, and any observations that stood out. Some days you may write detailed notes; other days maybe only a few words—both are valuable.

Every 10th day, you'll find a coaching checklist. These checklists offer structured guidance on what to look for as your train, plus helpful reminders and tips, so you can recognize progress and make thoughtful decisions about what to keep in mind or consider next. One special exception: Checklist #13 is about celebrating micro-wins, and it's there for you whenever you want a boost.

Using Initials

In veterinary medicine, we use initials to track who worked with an animal and how care progressed. You may choose to use initials in this logbook as well. This can be especially helpful for families or training teams, and many children enjoy initialing sessions as a way to feel involved and take ownership of their role in training.

Button training is a process that unfolds over time. Use this logbook to support that process, celebrate small wins, and stay connected to what your dog is communicating along the way.

Because every button press counts.

Date _______________

Pre-Training Mindset Checklist

Before you begin, ground yourself in realistic expectations.

☐ **Accept that progress takes time; each dog learns at their own pace.**
Small, steady steps are normal for every learner.

☐ **Focus on connection, not perfection.**
Your relationship matters more than flawless button presses.

☐ **Celebrate small wins — curiosity, sniffing, or glancing all count.**
Early interest builds motivation and confidence.

☐ **Ditch comparisons; your dog's journey will differ from every online video.**
Real life is slower, messier, and more meaningful.

☐ **Keep sessions short and positive.**
End while your dog is engaged and having fun.

Remember: buttons build trust — they don't replace love, walks, or play.
Approaching training with patience and perspective creates a smoother, more rewarding communication journey.

Date _____________________   Time________________

Dog's Name _______________________Temp_______

Room/Location_________________________________

Session Focus

☐ Introducing New Word(s) ☐ Reinforcing Words
☐ Observing Spontaneous Use ___________________
☐ Maintenance/Review ____________________________

Session Goals ________________________________

____

____

(e.g. Encourage independent use of "outside" button)

Buttons Used/Pressed

____

____

____

____

Observations and Insights

What went well today? ___________________________

____

____

____

What needs more practice? _______________________

____

____

Initials __________

This page is for notes—there's no 'right way' to fill it out.

Date_______________

1. What did your dog seem interested in or try today (buttons, words, sounds, or interactions)?

____

____

____

____

____

____

____

2. What stood out to you about today's session or time together?

____

____

____

____

____

____

____

Initials __________

Date _______________

1. What did you notice about your own timing, tone, or responses during the session?

2. Did the environment (location, button access, or distractions) seem to make communication easier or harder today?

____

____

____

____

____

____

____

____

____

____

____

____

Initials _________

Date _______________________   Time_________________

Dog's Name _______________________________Temp________

Room/Location____

Session Focus

☐ Introducing New Word(s) ☐ Reinforcing Words
☐ Observing Spontaneous Use _____________________
☐ Maintenance/Review _________________________________

Session Goals ______________________________________

____

____

(e.g. Encourage independent use of "outside" button)

Buttons Used/Pressed

____

____

____

____

Observations and Insights

What went well today? _________________________________

____

____

____

What needs more practice? _____________________________

____

____

Initials ___________

Date_________________

1. What responses to your training or modeling did you notice today (attention, pauses, repetition, frustration, confidence, curiosity)?

____

____

____

____

____

____

2. What choices did your dog make during the session (watching, approaching, pressing, repeating, stepping away)?

____

____

____

____

____

____

Initials _________

Date _________________

1. What learning patterns are you noticing in your dog over time?

2. Is there anything you'd like to keep doing or spend more time with in your next session?

____

____

____

____

____

____

____

____

____

____

____

____

____

Initials _________

Date ________________________   Time__________________

Dog's Name ___________________________Temp_______

Room/Location________________________________

Session Focus

☐ Introducing New Word(s) ☐ Reinforcing Words
☐ Observing Spontaneous Use ___________________
☐ Maintenance/Review _________________________

Session Goals _______________________________

____

____

(e.g. Encourage independent use of "outside" button)

Buttons Used/Pressed

____

____

____

____

Observations and Insights

What went well today? _________________________

____

____

____

What needs more practice? ______________________

____

____

Initials __________

Date_________________

1. What did your dog seem interested in or try today (buttons, words, sounds, or interactions)?

____

____

____

____

____

____

____

2. What stood out to you about today's session or time together?

____

____

____

____

____

____

____

Initials _________

Date _________________

1. What did you notice about your own timing,
tone, or responses during the session?

2. Did the environment (location, button access,
or distractions) seem to make communication
easier or harder today?

____

____

____

____

____

____

____

____

____

____

____

____

____

Initials _________

Date _____________

Choosing Your First Words Checklist

Run through this checklist before picking your starting words.

☐ **Does the word already elicit a clear reaction from my dog? Yes _____ No _____**

☐ **Can I practice this word several times daily? Yes ____ No ____**

☐ **When my dog uses this button, do I know what action to take? Yes ____ No ____**

☐ **Does my dog have specific behaviors tied to this word? Yes ____ No ____**
(For example: brings the leash for "walk," goes to the door for "outside," sits by the bowl for "water.")

☐ **Is this word easy and relevant for the whole household to reinforce? Yes ____ No ____**

If you answered yes to most of these, you've found solid candidates for your first set of buttons.

Date _____________________   Time_________________

Dog's Name _______________________________Temp_______

Room/Location____

Session Focus

☐ Introducing New Word(s) ☐ Reinforcing Words
☐ Observing Spontaneous Use _________________________
☐ Maintenance/Review ___________________________________

Session Goals ____

____

____

(e.g. Encourage independent use of "outside" button)

Buttons Used/Pressed

____

____

____

____

Observations and Insights

What went well today? _____________________________________

____

____

____

What needs more practice? _________________________________

____

____

Initials ____________

Date_______________

1. What responses to your training or modeling did you notice today (attention, pauses, repetition, frustration, confidence, curiosity)?

____

____

____

____

____

____

2. What choices did your dog make during the session (watching, approaching, pressing, repeating, stepping away)?

____

____

____

____

____

____

____

Initials __________

Date _______________

1. What learning patterns are you noticing in your dog over time?

2. Is there anything you'd like to keep doing or spend more time with next session?

____

____

____

____

____

____

____

____

____

____

____

____

____

Initials _________

Date _____________________   Time_________________

Dog's Name ______________________________Temp________

Room/Location____

Session Focus

☐ Introducing New Word(s) ☐ Reinforcing Words
☐ Observing Spontaneous Use _____________________
☐ Maintenance/Review ______________________________

Session Goals ____

____

____

(e.g. Encourage independent use of "outside" button)

Buttons Used/Pressed

____

____

____

____

Observations and Insights

What went well today? ___________________________________

____

____

____

What needs more practice? _______________________________

____

____

Initials ___________

Date________________

1. What did your dog seem interested in or try
today (buttons, words, sounds, or interactions)?

____

____

____

____

____

____

____

2. What stood out to you about today's session
or time together?

____

____

____

____

____

____

____

Initials _________

Date ______________

1. What did you notice about your own timing,
tone, or responses during the session?

2. Did the environment (location, button access,
or distractions) seem to make communication
easier or harder today?

Initials _________

Date _____________________   Time_________________

Dog's Name ________________________________Temp________

Room/Location_______________________________________

Session Focus

☐ Introducing New Word(s) ☐ Reinforcing Words
☐ Observing Spontaneous Use _____________________
☐ Maintenance/Review _________________________________

Session Goals ____

____

____

(e.g. Encourage independent use of "outside" button)

Buttons Used/Pressed

____

____

____

____

Observations and Insights

What went well today? ___________________________

____

____

____

What needs more practice? _______________________

____

____

Initials ___________

Date______________

1. What responses to your training or modeling
did you notice today (attention, pauses,
repetition, frustration, confidence, curiosity)?

____

____

____

____

____

____

____

2. What choices did your dog make during the
session (watching, approaching, pressing,
repeating, stepping away)?

____

____

____

____

____

____

____

Initials __________

Date _______________

1. What learning patterns are you noticing in your dog over time?

2. Is there anything you'd like to keep doing or spend more time with next session?

____

____

____

____

____

____

____

____

____

____

____

____

Initials _________

Date ________________

Button Placement Checklist

Before you begin modeling or recording, use this checklist to make sure your dog's buttons are placed where she can succeed—easy to reach, safe, and inviting to use.

☐ **Place buttons where they make sense.**
   For example, "outside" near the main door your dog uses most, or "eat" near the food bowl.

☐ **Choose calm locations.**
   Avoid hallways, cluttered rooms, and noisy areas like TVs or speakers.

☐ **If possible, make the board reachable from all directions.**
   Your dog should be able to approach the board several ways.

☐ **Adjust for size and mobility.**
   Small or older dogs may need a tilted or wall-mounted board; tall dogs, a low platform.

☐ **Be consistent.**
   Label each button's spot and always return the board to the same orientation.

☐ **Prevent slipping on smooth floors.**
   Use a non-skid rug for both your dog and the button board to prevent slipping.

☐ **Keep it clean and safe.**
   Keep buttons indoors, clean, and dry. Tidy cords and cables, and change batteries as needed.

☐ **Stay flexible.**
   Portable boards let you move key words around the house—or take them when you travel.

Setting your dog up with safe, sensible button placement ensures early success and builds confident communication from the very start.

Date ____________________   Time________________

Dog's Name ________________________Temp_______

Room/Location__________________________________

Session Focus

☐ Introducing New Word(s) ☐ Reinforcing Words
☐ Observing Spontaneous Use ___________________
☐ Maintenance/Review ______________________________

Session Goals _______________________________________

____

____

(e.g. Encourage independent use of "outside" button)

Buttons Used/Pressed

____

____

____

____

Observations and Insights

What went well today? ___________________________________

____

____

____

What needs more practice? _______________________________

____

____

Initials ___________

Date________________

1. What did your dog seem interested in or try
today (buttons, words, sounds, or interactions)?

____

____

____

____

____

____

2. What stood out to you about today's session
or time together?

____

____

____

____

____

____

Initials _________

Date _______________

1. What did you notice about your own timing, tone, or responses during the session?

2. Did the environment (location, button access, or distractions) seem to make communication easier or harder today?

Initials _________

Date _____________________   Time________________

Dog's Name _______________________Temp________

Room/Location_____________________________________

Session Focus

☐ Introducing New Word(s) ☐ Reinforcing Words
☐ Observing Spontaneous Use ___________________
☐ Maintenance/Review _______________________________

Session Goals ___________________________________

____

____

(e.g. Encourage independent use of "outside" button)

Buttons Used/Pressed

____

____

____

____

Observations and Insights

What went well today? _______________________________

____

____

____

What needs more practice? ___________________________

____

____

Initials ___________

Date_______________

1. What responses to your training or modeling did you notice today (attention, pauses, repetition, frustration, confidence, curiosity)?

____

____

____

____

____

____

2. What choices did your dog make during the session (watching, approaching, pressing, repeating, stepping away)?

____

____

____

____

____

____

Initials ________

Date ______________

1. What learning patterns are you noticing in your dog over time?

2. Is there anything you'd like to keep doing or spend more time with next session?

____

____

____

____

____

____

____

____

____

____

____

____

Initials ________

Date _____________________   Time_________________

Dog's Name _______________________Temp_______

Room/Location______________________________________

Session Focus

☐ Introducing New Word(s) ☐ Reinforcing Words
☐ Observing Spontaneous Use _________________
☐ Maintenance/Review ______________________________

Session Goals ____

____

____

(e.g. Encourage independent use of "outside" button)

Buttons Used/Pressed

____

____

____

____

Observations and Insights

What went well today? ______________________________

____

____

____

What needs more practice? __________________________

____

____

Initials ___________

Date_______________

1. What did your dog seem interested in or try today (buttons, words, sounds, or interactions)?

____

____

____

____

____

____

____

2. What stood out to you about today's session or time together?

____

____

____

____

____

____

____

Initials __________

Date _______________

1. What did you notice about your own timing,
tone, or responses during the session?

2. Did the environment (location, button access,
or distractions) seem to make communication
easier or harder today?

____

____

____

____

____

____

____

____

____

____

____

____

____

Initials _________

Date _________________

Engagement & Avoidance Checklist

Use this quick troubleshooting list to identify why your dog might be hesitant to approach or press his buttons.

☐ **Is the button accessible from your dog's favorite spot? Yes______ No ______**

☐ **Can your dog approach from multiple directions? Yes ______ No ______**

☐ **Is the area well-lit and roomy?**
Yes ______ No ______

☐ **Are you training when your dog is alert and calm? Yes ______ No ______**

☐ **Is the same person leading and using consistent cues? Yes ______ No ______**

☐ **Have you included engaging, meaningful words and activities? Yes ______ No ______**

☐ **Is the environment quiet and comfortable, with minimal distractions? Yes ______ No ______**

☐ **Are you changing only one thing at a time to monitor progress? Yes ______ No ______**

Each day, use this list to note what you adjust. Over time, patterns will emerge; certain times, locations, or activities that boost interest. This simple log helps you fine-tune consistency and make training more engaging.

Date ___________________   Time________________

Dog's Name ________________________Temp________

Room/Location_________________________________

Session Focus

☐ Introducing New Word(s) ☐ Reinforcing Words
☐ Observing Spontaneous Use ___________________
☐ Maintenance/Review _________________________

Session Goals _______________________________

____

____

(e.g. Encourage independent use of "outside" button)

Buttons Used/Pressed

____

____

____

____

Observations and Insights

What went well today? ___________________________

____

____

____

What needs more practice? _______________________

____

____

Initials ___________

Date______________

1. What responses to your training or modeling
did you notice today (attention, pauses,
repetition, frustration, confidence, curiosity)?

____

____

____

____

____

____

2. What choices did your dog make during the
session (watching, approaching, pressing,
repeating, stepping away)?

____

____

____

____

____

____

____

Initials __________

Date _______________

1. What learning patterns are you noticing in your dog over time?

2. Is there anything you'd like to keep doing or spend more time with next session?

____

____

____

____

____

____

____

____

____

____

____

____

____

Initials _________

Date _____________________   Time_________________

Dog's Name ______________________________Temp________

Room/Location____

Session Focus

☐ Introducing New Word(s) ☐ Reinforcing Words
☐ Observing Spontaneous Use _____________________
☐ Maintenance/Review ___________________________

Session Goals ______________________________________

____

____

(e.g. Encourage independent use of "outside" button)

Buttons Used/Pressed

____

____

____

____

Observations and Insights

What went well today? _________________________

____

____

____

What needs more practice? _____________________

____

____

Initials ___________

Date________________

1. What did your dog seem interested in or try today (buttons, words, sounds, or interactions)?

____

____

____

____

____

____

____

2. What stood out to you about today's session or time together?

____

____

____

____

____

____

____

Initials _________

Date ________________

1. What did you notice about your own timing, tone, or responses during the session?

2. Did the environment (location, button access, or distractions) seem to make communication easier or harder today?

____

____

____

____

____

____

____

____

____

____

____

____

Initials _________

Date ___________________________   Time__________________

Dog's Name ____________________________Temp_______

Room/Location_______________________________________

Session Focus

☐ Introducing New Word(s) ☐ Reinforcing Words
☐ Observing Spontaneous Use ___________________
☐ Maintenance/Review ___________________________

Session Goals ________________________________

____

____

(e.g. Encourage independent use of "outside" button)

Buttons Used/Pressed

____

____

____

____

Observations and Insights

What went well today? _______________________

____

____

____

What needs more practice? ___________________

____

____

Initials __________

Date_______________

1. What responses to your training or modeling
did you notice today (attention, pauses,
repetition, frustration, confidence, curiosity)?

____

____

____

____

____

____

2. What choices did your dog make during the
session (watching, approaching, pressing,
repeating, stepping away)?

____

____

____

____

____

____

Initials _________

Date ______________

1. What learning patterns are you noticing in your dog over time?

2. Is there anything you'd like to keep doing or spend more time with next session?

____

____

____

____

____

____

____

____

____

____

____

____

____

Initials _________

Date ________________

Adding Successful New Words Checklist

Consider each question before choosing your dog's next new word(s).

☐ **Does my dog often express this need or behavior? Yes _____ No _____**

☐ **Can I consistently follow through when my dog uses this word? Yes _____ No _____**

☐ **Does this word meet a need or bring my dog joy? Yes _____ No _____**

☐ **Will all household members recognize and reinforce the word? Yes _____ No _____**

☐ **Will this word increase engagement or reduce frustration? Yes _____ No _____**

Using this worksheet keeps your new button choices thoughtful, consistent, and grounded in real daily routines. Keep this worksheet handy—your dog's vocabulary grows most naturally when real life sets the pace.

By observing, balancing needs and wants, and involving your household, you'll build a practical, joyful board that fits your dog's personality and enriches communication every day.

Date _______________________   Time_________________

Dog's Name _______________________________Temp_______

Room/Location____

Session Focus

☐ Introducing New Word(s) ☐ Reinforcing Words
☐ Observing Spontaneous Use _____________________
☐ Maintenance/Review _________________________________

Session Goals ____

____

____

(e.g. Encourage independent use of "outside" button)

Buttons Used/Pressed

____

____

____

____

Observations and Insights

What went well today? ___________________________________

____

____

____

What needs more practice? _______________________________

____

____

Initials ___________

Date_______________

1. What did your dog seem interested in or try
today (buttons, words, sounds, or interactions)?

____

____

____

____

____

____

____

2. What stood out to you about today's session
or time together?

____

____

____

____

____

____

____

Initials _________

Date _________________

1. What did you notice about your own timing,
tone, or responses during the session?

2. Did the environment (location, button access,
or distractions) seem to make communication
easier or harder today?

____

____

____

____

____

____

____

____

____

____

____

____

____

Initials _________

Date _____________________________   Time_____________________

Dog's Name ________________________________Temp_________

Room/Location____

Session Focus

☐ Introducing New Word(s) ☐ Reinforcing Words
☐ Observing Spontaneous Use _____________________________
☐ Maintenance/Review ________________________________

Session Goals ____

____

____

(e.g. Encourage independent use of "outside" button)

Buttons Used/Pressed

____

____

____

____

Observations and Insights

What went well today? ___________________________________

____

____

____

What needs more practice? _______________________________

____

____

Initials ____________

Date_______________

1. What responses to your training or modeling did you notice today (attention, pauses, repetition, frustration, confidence, curiosity)?

____

____

____

____

____

____

2. What choices did your dog make during the session (watching, approaching, pressing, repeating, stepping away)?

____

____

____

____

____

____

Initials _________

Date _________________

1. What learning patterns are you noticing in your dog over time?

2. Is there anything you'd like to keep doing or spend more time with next session?

____

____

____

____

____

____

____

____

____

____

____

____

____

Initials __________

Date _______________________   Time_______________

Dog's Name _______________________________Temp_______

Room/Location____

Session Focus

☐ Introducing New Word(s) ☐ Reinforcing Words
☐ Observing Spontaneous Use _______________________
☐ Maintenance/Review _________________________________

Session Goals ______________________________________

____

____

(e.g. Encourage independent use of "outside" button)

Buttons Used/Pressed

____

____

____

____

Observations and Insights

What went well today? __________________________________

____

____

____

What needs more practice? ______________________________

____

____

Initials ____________

Date________________

1. What did your dog seem interested in or try today (buttons, words, sounds, or interactions)?

____

____

____

____

____

____

2. What stood out to you about today's session or time together?

____

____

____

____

____

____

Initials __________

Date _____________

1. What did you notice about your own timing, tone, or responses during the session?

2. Did the environment (location, button access, or distractions) seem to make communication easier or harder today?

Initials ________

Date _____________

Troubleshooting Checklist: When Words Get Mixed Up

Use this quick guide to strengthen clarity before adding more words.

☐ **Do recorded words sound too similar?**

☐ **Were related words introduced at the same time?**

☐ **Has enough practice time passed before adding a similar-sounding or similar-meaning word?**

☐ **Is your button board labeled so buttons can be returned to the correct spots if they get moved or displaced?**

Checking these points restores clarity and keeps communication frustration-free.

Date _____________________   Time__________________

Dog's Name _______________________________Temp_______

Room/Location_____________________________________

Session Focus

☐ Introducing New Word(s) ☐ Reinforcing Words
☐ Observing Spontaneous Use _____________________
☐ Maintenance/Review _________________________________

Session Goals _____________________________________

____

____

(e.g. Encourage independent use of "outside" button)

Buttons Used/Pressed

____

____

____

____

Observations and Insights

What went well today? _________________________________

____

____

____

What needs more practice? _____________________________

____

____

Initials ____________

Date________________

1. What responses to your training or modeling did you notice today (attention, pauses, repetition, frustration, confidence, curiosity)?

____

____

____

____

____

____

2. What choices did your dog make during the session (watching, approaching, pressing, repeating, stepping away)?

____

____

____

____

____

____

Initials __________

Date _______________

1. What learning patterns are you noticing in your dog over time?

2. Is there anything you'd like to keep doing or spend more time with next session?

____

____

____

____

____

____

____

____

____

____

____

____

Initials _________

Date _____________________   Time_______________

Dog's Name _______________________Temp_______

Room/Location_________________________________

Session Focus

☐ Introducing New Word(s) ☐ Reinforcing Words
☐ Observing Spontaneous Use _____________________
☐ Maintenance/Review _________________________

Session Goals _________________________________

____

____

(e.g. Encourage independent use of "outside" button)

Buttons Used/Pressed

____

____

____

____

Observations and Insights

What went well today? _______________________

____

____

____

What needs more practice? ____________________

____

____

Initials __________

Date________________

1. What did your dog seem interested in or try
today (buttons, words, sounds, or interactions)?

____

____

____

____

____

____

____

2. What stood out to you about today's session
or time together?

____

____

____

____

____

____

____

Initials __________

Date _______________

1. What did you notice about your own timing, tone, or responses during the session?

2. Did the environment (location, button access, or distractions) seem to make communication easier or harder today?

____

Initials _________

Date ___________________________   Time________________

Dog's Name ___________________________Temp_______

Room/Location___________________________________

Session Focus

☐ Introducing New Word(s) ☐ Reinforcing Words
☐ Observing Spontaneous Use ___________________
☐ Maintenance/Review ______________________________

Session Goals ______________________________________

____

____

(e.g. Encourage independent use of "outside" button)

Buttons Used/Pressed

____

____

____

____

Observations and Insights

What went well today? _________________________________

____

____

____

What needs more practice? _____________________________

____

____

Initials ___________

Date________________

1. What responses to your training or modeling
did you notice today (attention, pauses,
repetition, frustration, confidence, curiosity)?

____

____

____

____

____

____

2. What choices did your dog make during the
session (watching, approaching, pressing,
repeating, stepping away)?

____

____

____

____

____

____

Initials __________

Date ______________

1. What learning patterns are you noticing in your dog over time?

2. Is there anything you'd like to keep doing or spend more time with next session?

____

____

____

____

____

____

____

____

____

____

____

____

____

Initials ________

Date _______________

Puppy Button Training Checklist

Use this checklist to integrate buttons smoothly during early learning.

☐ **Does your puppy hear each button sound at least twice a day? Yes _____ No _____**

☐ **Are presses paired with praise, play, or meaningful actions? Yes _____ No _____**

☐ **Are sessions kept short (2–3 minutes) and fun? Yes _____ No _____**

☐ **Are you keeping a simple, consistent log of your puppy's button use? Yes _____ No _____**

If you answered mostly "yes," you're building a solid foundation for long-term communication.

Date _____________________   Time_______________

Dog's Name _______________________Temp_______

Room/Location_______________________________

Session Focus

☐ Introducing New Word(s) ☐ Reinforcing Words
☐ Observing Spontaneous Use _____________________
☐ Maintenance/Review _______________________________

Session Goals _________________________________

____

____

(e.g. Encourage independent use of "outside" button)

Buttons Used/Pressed

____

____

____

____

Observations and Insights

What went well today? ____________________________

____

____

____

What needs more practice? ________________________

____

____

Initials ___________

Date________________

1. What did your dog seem interested in or try
today (buttons, words, sounds, or interactions)?

____

____

____

____

____

____

2. What stood out to you about today's session
or time together?

____

____

____

____

____

____

Initials _________

Date ______________

1. What did you notice about your own timing,
tone, or responses during the session?

2. Did the environment (location, button access,
or distractions) seem to make communication
easier or harder today?

____

____

____

____

____

____

____

____

____

____

____

____

____

Initials _________

Date ___________________________   Time________________

Dog's Name _________________________Temp_______

Room/Location__________________________________

Session Focus

☐ Introducing New Word(s) ☐ Reinforcing Words
☐ Observing Spontaneous Use ___________________
☐ Maintenance/Review ____________________________

Session Goals ________________________________

____

____

(e.g. Encourage independent use of "outside" button)

Buttons Used/Pressed

____

____

____

____

Observations and Insights

What went well today? ___________________________

____

____

____

What needs more practice? _______________________

____

____

Initials ___________

Date_______________

1. What responses to your training or modeling did you notice today (attention, pauses, repetition, frustration, confidence, curiosity)?

____

____

____

____

____

____

2. What choices did your dog make during the session (watching, approaching, pressing, repeating, stepping away)?

____

____

____

____

____

____

Initials _________

Date _______________

1. What learning patterns are you noticing in your dog over time?

2. Is there anything you'd like to keep doing or spend more time with next session?

____

____

____

____

____

____

____

____

____

____

____

____

____

Initials _________

Date _____________________   Time_________________

Dog's Name _______________________________Temp________

Room/Location____

Session Focus

- ☐ Introducing New Word(s) ☐ Reinforcing Words
- ☐ Observing Spontaneous Use _____________________
- ☐ Maintenance/Review _________________________

Session Goals _______________________________________

____

____

(e.g. Encourage independent use of "outside" button)

Buttons Used/Pressed

____

____

____

____

Observations and Insights

What went well today? _________________________________

____

____

____

What needs more practice? _____________________________

____

____

Initials ___________

Date_______________

1. What did your dog seem interested in or try
today (buttons, words, sounds, or interactions)?

____

____

____

____

____

____

____

2. What stood out to you about today's session
or time together?

____

____

____

____

____

____

____

Initials _________

Date _______________

1. What did you notice about your own timing,
tone, or responses during the session?

2. Did the environment (location, button access,
or distractions) seem to make communication
easier or harder today?

____

____

____

____

____

____

____

____

____

____

____

____

Initials _________

Date _________________

Senior Dog Communication Checklist

Use this checklist to support your senior's comfort and confidence:

☐ **Are the buttons placed near your dog's favorite resting spot? Yes _____ No _____**

☐ **Is the board raised, angled, or mounted at a height that's easy for their paws or nose nudges? Yes _____ No _____**

☐ **Do the buttons stay stable with non-slip backing or Velcro? Yes _____ No _____**

☐ **Are pathways to the board clear and uncluttered? Yes _____ No _____**

☐ **Do you allow extra time after modeling a word before expecting a response? Yes _____ No _____**

☐ **Are training sessions short, calm, and free from distractions? Yes _____ No _____**

☐ **Is your senior getting quiet practice time without younger dogs crowding in? Yes _____ No _____**

☐ **Are you celebrating small wins and noting moments of interest or effort? Yes _____ No _____**

Every thoughtful choice you make supports your senior's ability to communicate in ways that honor her age and abilities.

Date _______________________   Time__________________

Dog's Name _______________________Temp______

Room/Location______________________________

Session Focus

☐ Introducing New Word(s) ☐ Reinforcing Words
☐ Observing Spontaneous Use ___________________
☐ Maintenance/Review ______________________________

Session Goals ______________________________

____

____

(e.g. Encourage independent use of "outside" button)

Buttons Used/Pressed

____

____

____

____

Observations and Insights

What went well today? ___________________________

____

____

____

What needs more practice? _______________________

____

____

Initials __________

Date_______________

1. What responses to your training or modeling
did you notice today (attention, pauses,
repetition, frustration, confidence, curiosity)?

____

____

____

____

____

____

2. What choices did your dog make during the
session (watching, approaching, pressing,
repeating, stepping away)?

____

____

____

____

____

____

____

Initials _________

Date ______________

1. What learning patterns are you noticing in your dog over time?

2. Is there anything you'd like to keep doing or spend more time with next session?

____

____

____

____

____

____

____

____

____

____

____

____

____

Initials _________

Date _____________________   Time_________________

Dog's Name ______________________________Temp_______

Room/Location____

Session Focus

☐ Introducing New Word(s) ☐ Reinforcing Words
☐ Observing Spontaneous Use _____________________
☐ Maintenance/Review ___________________________

Session Goals ____________________________________

____

____

(e.g. Encourage independent use of "outside" button)

Buttons Used/Pressed

____

____

____

____

Observations and Insights

What went well today? _______________________________

____

____

____

What needs more practice? ___________________________

____

____

Initials __________

Date________________

1. What did your dog seem interested in or try today (buttons, words, sounds, or interactions)?

____

____

____

____

____

____

____

2. What stood out to you about today's session or time together?

____

____

____

____

____

____

____

Initials _________

Date _______________

1. What did you notice about your own timing,
tone, or responses during the session?

2. Did the environment (location, button access,
or distractions) seem to make communication
easier or harder today?

____

____

____

____

____

____

____

____

____

____

____

____

____

Initials _________

Date _____________________   Time_________________

Dog's Name ______________________________Temp_______

Room/Location____

Session Focus

☐ Introducing New Word(s) ☐ Reinforcing Words
☐ Observing Spontaneous Use _____________________
☐ Maintenance/Review _________________________________

Session Goals _____________________________________

____

____

(e.g. Encourage independent use of "outside" button)

Buttons Used/Pressed

____

____

____

____

Observations and Insights

What went well today? _______________________________

____

____

____

What needs more practice? ___________________________

____

____

Initials ___________

Date_______________

1. What responses to your training or modeling did you notice today (attention, pauses, repetition, frustration, confidence, curiosity)?

____

____

____

____

____

____

2. What choices did your dog make during the session (watching, approaching, pressing, repeating, stepping away)?

____

____

____

____

____

____

Initials _________

Date _______________

1. What learning patterns are you noticing in your dog over time?

2. Is there anything you'd like to keep doing or spend more time with next session?

____

____

____

____

____

____

____

____

____

____

____

____

____

Initials _________

Date ________________

Reflection Exercise Checklist:
Button Fatigue Self-Check

Once a week, take a few minutes to review:

☐ **Is my dog acting uninterested (walking away, avoiding the board)? Yes _____ No _____**

☐ **Am I bored, impatient, or stressed during training? Yes _____ No _____**

☐ **Did we include at least one "button-free" day this week? Yes _____ No _____**

☐ **Did I use a variety of rewards—praise, play, or other activities? Yes _____ No _____**

☐ **Were all sessions under ten minutes? Yes _____ No _____**

☐ **Have I talked with my family about what's working and what's not? Yes _____ No _____**

☐**Are sessions happening during our natural high-energy times? Yes _____ No _____**

If even one answer is "no," take it as a cue to adjust your pace this week—more rest, shorter sessions, or a slight shift in routine.

Date _______________________   Time__________________

Dog's Name ________________________________Temp________

Room/Location____

Session Focus

☐ Introducing New Word(s) ☐ Reinforcing Words
☐ Observing Spontaneous Use _______________________
☐ Maintenance/Review _______________________________

Session Goals ____

____

____

(e.g. Encourage independent use of "outside" button)

Buttons Used/Pressed

____

____

____

____

Observations and Insights

What went well today? ___________________________________

____

____

____

What needs more practice? _______________________________

____

____

Initials ___________

Date______________

1. What did your dog seem interested in or try
today (buttons, words, sounds, or interactions)?

____

____

____

____

____

____

____

2. What stood out to you about today's session
or time together?

____

____

____

____

____

____

____

Initials __________

Date _______________

1. What did you notice about your own timing, tone, or responses during the session?

2. Did the environment (location, button access, or distractions) seem to make communication easier or harder today?

Initials _________

Date _____________________   Time_______________

Dog's Name _______________________Temp_______

Room/Location____________________________________

Session Focus

☐ Introducing New Word(s) ☐ Reinforcing Words
☐ Observing Spontaneous Use   _________________
☐ Maintenance/Review _______________________

Session Goals _______________________________

____

____

(e.g. Encourage independent use of "outside" button)

Buttons Used/Pressed

____

____

____

____

Observations and Insights

What went well today? ___________________________

____

____

____

What needs more practice? _______________________

____

____

Initials __________

Date________________

1. What responses to your training or modeling did you notice today (attention, pauses, repetition, frustration, confidence, curiosity)?

____

____

____

____

____

____

2. What choices did your dog make during the session (watching, approaching, pressing, repeating, stepping away)?

____

____

____

____

____

____

____

Initials _________

Date _________________

1. What learning patterns are you noticing in your dog over time?

2. Is there anything you'd like to keep doing or spend more time with next session?

____

____

____

____

____

____

____

____

____

____

____

____

____

Initials _________

Date _____________________   Time_________________

Dog's Name _______________________Temp_______

Room/Location_____________________________________

Session Focus

☐ Introducing New Word(s) ☐ Reinforcing Words
☐ Observing Spontaneous Use _____________________
☐ Maintenance/Review _________________________________

Session Goals ____

____

____

(e.g. Encourage independent use of "outside" button)

Buttons Used/Pressed

____

____

____

____

Observations and Insights

What went well today? ___________________________________

____

____

____

What needs more practice? _______________________________

____

____

Initials ___________

Date_______________

1. What did your dog seem interested in or try today (buttons, words, sounds, or interactions)?

____

____

____

____

____

____

____

2. What stood out to you about today's session or time together?

____

____

____

____

____

____

Initials _________

Date _______________

1. What did you notice about your own timing, tone, or responses during the session?

2. Did the environment (location, button access, or distractions) seem to make communication easier or harder today?

____

Initials _________

Date ________________

Intent Checklist: How to Know When He Really Means It

Use this checklist to help gauge intent and guide your responses. Did your dog:

☐ **Press the same button three or more times in a consistent context? Yes _____ No _____**

☐ **Make eye contact or show focused posture before or after pressing? Yes _____ No _____**

☐ **Follow up with behavior that matched the request (e.g., go to the door after "outside" press)?**
Yes _____ No _____

☐ **Show emotional cues—tail wag, whining, pacing?**
Yes _____ No _____

☐ **Persist—repeat the press when ignored?**
Yes _____ No _____

☐ **Wait for a contextually relevant second press when needed Yes _____ No _____**

Use this checklist to decode intent, support your dog's confidence, and strengthen your growing communication partnership.

Date _____________________   Time_____________________

Dog's Name _______________________________Temp________

Room/Location____

Session Focus

☐ Introducing New Word(s) ☐ Reinforcing Words
☐ Observing Spontaneous Use _____________________
☐ Maintenance/Review _________________________________

Session Goals ____

____

____

(e.g. Encourage independent use of "outside" button)

Buttons Used/Pressed

____

____

____

____

Observations and Insights

What went well today? _________________________________

____

____

____

What needs more practice? _____________________________

____

____

Initials ___________

Date_______________

1. What responses to your training or modeling did you notice today (attention, pauses, repetition, frustration, confidence, curiosity)?

____

____

____

____

____

____

2. What choices did your dog make during the session (watching, approaching, pressing, repeating, stepping away)?

____

____

____

____

____

____

Initials _________

Date _______________

1. What learning patterns are you noticing in your dog over time?

2. Is there anything you'd like to keep doing or spend more time with next session?

____

____

____

____

____

____

____

____

____

____

____

____

____

Initials _________

Date _____________________   Time__________________

Dog's Name ________________________________Temp________

Room/Location____

Session Focus

☐ Introducing New Word(s) ☐ Reinforcing Words
☐ Observing Spontaneous Use ____________________
☐ Maintenance/Review ______________________________

Session Goals ____________________________________

____

____

(e.g. Encourage independent use of "outside" button)

Buttons Used/Pressed

____

____

____

____

Observations and Insights

What went well today? ______________________________

____

____

____

What needs more practice? ___________________________

____

____

Initials ___________

Date________________

1. What did your dog seem interested in or try today (buttons, words, sounds, or interactions)?

____

____

____

____

____

____

2. What stood out to you about today's session or time together?

____

____

____

____

____

____

Initials _________

Date _______________

1. What did you notice about your own timing,
tone, or responses during the session?

2. Did the environment (location, button access,
or distractions) seem to make communication
easier or harder today?

____

____

____

____

____

____

____

____

____

____

____

____

____

Initials _________

Date ________________________   Time__________________

Dog's Name ____________________________Temp_______

Room/Location____________________________________

Session Focus

☐ Introducing New Word(s) ☐ Reinforcing Words
☐ Observing Spontaneous Use ___________________
☐ Maintenance/Review _________________________

Session Goals __________________________________

____

____

(e.g. Encourage independent use of "outside" button)

Buttons Used/Pressed

____

____

____

____

Observations and Insights

What went well today? ____________________________

____

____

____

What needs more practice? __________________________

____

____

Initials ___________

Date________________

1. What responses to your training or modeling did you notice today (attention, pauses, repetition, frustration, confidence, curiosity)?

____

____

____

____

____

____

2. What choices did your dog make during the session (watching, approaching, pressing, repeating, stepping away)?

____

____

____

____

____

____

Initials _________

Date _______________

1. What learning patterns are you noticing in your dog over time?

2. Is there anything you'd like to keep doing or spend more time with next session?

____

____

____

____

____

____

____

____

____

____

____

____

____

Initials _________

Date _________________

Routine Maintenance Checklist

Use this list for a simple routine that keeps your dog's buttons working well.

☐ **Wipe surfaces every 2–3 days if they're accumulating dirt**

☐ **Deep-clean after outdoor or messy use**

☐ **Clear debris under mats weekly**

☐ **Replace or recharge batteries when buttons show signs of battery fatigue, such as muffled sound or slow playback.**
(Depending on your dog's button use, monthly may be a good interval.)

☐ **Store and recycle batteries safely and responsibly**

☐ **Keep buttons dry and out of direct heat or sun**

☐ **Encourage gentle presses**

☐ **Replace buttons that fail after cleaning**

Consistent care keeps your dog's communication clear, reliable, and frustration-free.

Date _____________________   Time_________________

Dog's Name ______________________________Temp________

Room/Location_______________________________________

Session Focus

☐ Introducing New Word(s) ☐ Reinforcing Words
☐ Observing Spontaneous Use _____________________
☐ Maintenance/Review _________________________________

Session Goals ____

____

____

(e.g. Encourage independent use of "outside" button)

Buttons Used/Pressed

____

____

____

____

Observations and Insights

What went well today? _____________________________________

____

____

____

What needs more practice? _________________________________

____

____

Initials ___________

Date________________

1. What did your dog seem interested in or try today (buttons, words, sounds, or interactions)?

____

____

____

____

____

____

____

2. What stood out to you about today's session or time together?

____

____

____

____

____

____

Initials __________

Date _______________

1. What did you notice about your own timing, tone, or responses during the session?

2. Did the environment (location, button access, or distractions) seem to make communication easier or harder today?

Initials _________

Date _______________________   Time_________________

Dog's Name ___________________________Temp________

Room/Location___________________________________

Session Focus

☐ Introducing New Word(s) ☐ Reinforcing Words
☐ Observing Spontaneous Use ____________________
☐ Maintenance/Review ______________________________

Session Goals _______________________________________

____

____

(e.g. Encourage independent use of "outside" button)

Buttons Used/Pressed

____

____

____

____

Observations and Insights

What went well today? ___________________________________

____

____

____

What needs more practice? _______________________________

____

____

Initials ___________

Date______________

1. What responses to your training or modeling did you notice today (attention, pauses, repetition, frustration, confidence, curiosity)?

____

____

____

____

____

____

2. What choices did your dog make during the session (watching, approaching, pressing, repeating, stepping away)?

____

____

____

____

____

____

Initials __________

Date ________________

1. What learning patterns are you noticing in your dog over time?

2. Is there anything you'd like to keep doing or spend more time with next session?

____

____

____

____

____

____

____

____

____

____

____

____

____

Initials __________

Date _____________________   Time________________

Dog's Name ___________________________Temp_______

Room/Location____

Session Focus

☐ Introducing New Word(s) ☐ Reinforcing Words
☐ Observing Spontaneous Use ___________________
☐ Maintenance/Review _________________________________

Session Goals ____

____

____

(e.g. Encourage independent use of "outside" button)

Buttons Used/Pressed

____

____

____

____

Observations and Insights

What went well today? _____________________________

____

____

____

What needs more practice? ________________________

____

____

Initials __________

Date________________

1. What did your dog seem interested in or try
today (buttons, words, sounds, or interactions)?

____

____

____

____

____

____

____

2. What stood out to you about today's session
or time together?

____

____

____

____

____

____

____

Initials __________

Date _______________

1. What did you notice about your own timing, tone, or responses during the session?

2. Did the environment (location, button access, or distractions) seem to make communication easier or harder today?

____

____

____

____

____

____

____

____

____

____

____

____

Initials _________

Date _________________

Intermediate Talker Checklist—Is Your Dog Ready For More Words?

Add new words when your dog is ready and the situation calls for them.

☐ **They regularly use most of the words they already have. Yes _____ No _____**

☐ **They use some words but avoid others. Yes _____ No _____**

☐ **They've started combining words. Yes _____ No _____**

☐ **They seem frustrated around the board. Yes _____ No _____**
(This can indicate they want to use words they don't have yet.)

☐ **There's a change in routine or environment. Yes _____ No _____**
(Again, this can indicate they want to use words that describe their new circumstances.)

They may surprise you with just how creatively they use their expanding language.

Date _____________________   Time_________________

Dog's Name ______________________________Temp_______

Room/Location____

Session Focus

☐ Introducing New Word(s) ☐ Reinforcing Words
☐ Observing Spontaneous Use _________________
☐ Maintenance/Review _________________________

Session Goals ___________________________________

____

____

(e.g. Encourage independent use of "outside" button)

Buttons Used/Pressed

____

____

____

____

Observations and Insights

What went well today? _______________________

____

____

____

What needs more practice? ___________________

____

____

Initials __________

Date________________

1. What responses to your training or modeling did you notice today (attention, pauses, repetition, frustration, confidence, curiosity)?

____

____

____

____

____

____

2. What choices did your dog make during the session (watching, approaching, pressing, repeating, stepping away)?

____

____

____

____

____

____

Initials __________

Date _______________

1. What learning patterns are you noticing in your dog over time?

2. Is there anything you'd like to keep doing or spend more time with next session?

____

____

____

____

____

____

____

____

____

____

____

____

____

Initials _________

Date _____________

Celebration Ideas For Button Training

Meaningful Ways to Celebrate Button Milestones

☐ **Print a certificate for your dog's newest word or milestone**

☐ **Give a "milestone toy" or extra-special chew or game**

☐ **Have a family "button cake" night** *(dog gets a safe treat, humans get dessert)*

☐ **Build a milestone photo wall or collage near the button board**

☐ **Let kids design badges, stickers, or tiny awards**

☐ **Throw a small "button party"** *(even simple hats and extra playtime count)*

☐ **Create an indoor "word garden" bowl and add a decorated rock—painted, colored, or embellished with stickers or words—for each new word**

☐ **Share a progress photo or video with friends or your training community**

☐ **Start a group text or video call so loved ones can celebrate breakthroughs with you**

Whether a milestone is big or small, celebrating it helps keep the journey joyful and meaningful.

A Small Request

If this logbook supported you — by helping you notice progress, stay consistent, or better understand your dog —please consider leaving a brief review.

Reviews will help other dog owners find this logbook to support them along their button training journey.

To leave a review:

Scan the QR code below:

Thank you for helping other dogs find their words and communicate more fully with the people who love them.

— Karen E. Mueller, DVM

A Special Gift for Your Button Journey

Training with buttons is full of small moments that matter — curiosity, surprise, pride. To support you along the way, I've created a free bonus resource to use alongside this logbook.

On my website, you'll find a special gift created specifically for families using this logbook. It's designed to support your practice, spark confidence, and help you keep moving forward, especially on days when progress feels subtle.

This bonus may include things like:
- Sample log entries and real-world examples
- Gentle guidance for common "what now?" moments
- Tips for staying consistent without pressure
- Certificates and badges to celebrate your micro-wins and successes

This resource is meant to complement your book and logbook — not replace them. It focuses on insight, reassurance, and perspective rather than practice pages. Many families use it as a light touchpoint between training sessions or when they want a little extra encouragement.

To access your gift, visit:

https://kmuellerpublishing.com

Thank you for being curious, patient, and willing to listen closely to your dog. Those qualities matter more than perfection — and they're what make communication grow.

— Karen E. Mueller, DVM

Also by Karen E. Mueller, DVM

Animal Communication & Behavior: Teach Them to Talk™ Series

Coming Soon:

Teach Your Cat to Talk: A Practical Guide to Button Training for Cats

Cat Button Training Logbook:
Track Your Cat's Words, Progress, and Milestones—A companion journal to
Teach Your Cat to Talk

Humor & Parenting: Some Things Suck™ Series

Some Moms Suck Way More Than You: 24 Animal Parenting Fails That Prove You're NOT a Bad Mom

Some Dads Suck Way More Than You: 22 Wild Examples That Prove Why You're a Great Dad

Cryptozoology & Natural History: Creatures of the World™ Series

Cryptid Creatures of the World: An Illustrated Guide to Myths, Monsters, and Mysterious Creatures Haunting Six Continents

Criaturas Críptidas del Mundo: Una Guía Ilustrada de Mitos, Monstruos y Criaturas Misteriosas que Habitan en los Seis Continentes

Cryptids of the World: Where Legends Meet Reality

Críptidos del Mundo, Donde las Leyendas se Encuentran con la Realidad

Sasquatch: Insights into Their Lives and Encounters with Humans